IN THE SWEETNESS

OF THE NEW TIME

Henry Weinfield

HOUSE OF KEYS

Atlanta . Georgia

ACKNOWLEDGMENTS

These poems were originally published in the following magazines and anthologies:

Balaam's Ass, Centerpoint, Choice, Daimon, Endymion, First Issue, Loose Change, Made In Canada, The Mysterious Barricades, Penumbra, Poetry (Chicago), *Promethean, Rozinante.*

"Passacaille" first appeared in *The Carnival Cantata*, Unicorn Press, Santa Barbara, California. Copyright: Henry Weinfield, 1971.

Produced at The Print Center, Inc., Box 1050, Brooklyn, N.Y., 11202, a non-profit printing facility for literary and arts-related publications. Funded by The New York State Council on the Arts and the National Endowment for the Arts.

To whom, quoth the Nightingale, shall these songs be sung?
To the Forest of Strangers and at last to the Wind.

CONTENTS

I. THE FOREST OF STRANGERS

II. GRAMMATICAL VERSES

ENVOI

THE FOREST OF STRANGERS

GRADUS AD PARNASSUM

Gradus ad Parnassum,
The man in the moon
Said nothing about the case
Because he was / the case.

His letters were signed to unknown persons,
And the sea was all his cathedrals.
He neither tangled in the stars,
Nor whirled the flaming dervish of the sun.

He had a dream
"That was not all a dream";
He walked upon the waves.
But when they sang
A certain song,
He walked among the dead.

A battle was turned to a dance,
But all the people were sad.
And all the people are sad?

The sea was all his cathedrals.

WALKING TO BUXTEHUDE

Many miles walking to Buxtehude
            over the barley fields
            a painting by Breughel,
And singing of silence, this city is silent,
The organ goes straight through my soul.

Walking in allegory, walking to Buxtehude
            over the barley fields
            or else Timbuktoo
Where peasants are weary, for I, in the allegory,
Shall sleep in the arms of his passionate daughter.

Many years later, walking to Buxtehude
            over the barley fields
            defunct as the soul
That slept in the arms of the passionate organ,
The passionate daughter goes straight through my soul.

THE SOLDIER, THE SOLITARY,

THE AMATEUR, THE RAKE

The soldier, the solitary, the amateur, the rake—
All of these men were in love with you.
Were they known to you? did you know them?
They have merged themselves inside of you,
Dancer that balanced their days.

The soldier, the solitary, the amateur, the rake
Are eager men. They would kill you
Not only with their hate.
Wanting your flesh, their blood is shrill,
They want it over, this loneliest dance.

A birth, a death, they say, who knows
The man of sorrows, of infinite change?
Here, the pirouette: moment of departure,
A slender acquiescence for the fluttering swan
When the brazen blacksmith pounds the anvil.

Shall love be adulterous, and shall the night
Be known by the sorrowful makers of song?
We are singing a song of no birth, no becoming:
We sing, we are singing, we may not awake
The soldier, the solitary, the amateur, the rake.

THE LAWS OF THE MEDES AND PERSIANS

The sky would be red
would be crimson and scarlet
(the gulls of the sea)

The ferry that never
encountered the shore.
The boatman would sing
if he understood song:

And I too am happy
And I too am happy

The sky would be red
would be crimson and scarlet
(the gulls of the sea)

PRELIMINARY COURSE OF STUDY

When you master the lute
you shall put out to sea
to study the art
of touching the clavier.

By flutes you shall come
to a barbarous land
where an Irish bassoon
holds the people in thrall.

My lord, wit you well,
you shall cut off his head;
which thing being done,
to the Dolorous Wood

(hautboy) you'll repair.
When the Nightingale sings
of my lady Iseult
whom the clarion calls,

you shall study that song
till it flows in your blood;
my lord, wit you well,
till it flows in the sea.

SLOW STEPS / THE MUDDY SHORE

slow steps,
the muddy shore:
a silhouette
upon the road.

He left his lamp
upon the sand;
he left his nets
upon the sea.

He left the face
the world had changed:
the world has changed,
has changed
has changed.

SARABANDE

They never laugh, for whom smiles are eternal,
For the angels have riveted their faces
That they no longer / leap into the air;
They are never,
They never dance with the old fever.

LE TOMBEAU DE COUPERIN

I. PASSACAILLE

The march through the woods is a grand passacaglia
For the huntsman, the stag and the solemn crusader.

Do you think the march is long?
The march is long, smiled the sky, and a grief-wizened tree
smiled, but the march is short
For the black-eyed fawn and his charming mother.

Shall an arrow pierce her elegant neck,
noble lords and ladies?
Who will bear homeward the radiant prize,
grave and ponderous crusaders?
What spoils will you steal
from the sky?
And what is this lust to be real?
Do you understand my laughter?

For the huntsman, the stag, the solemn crusader,
The march through the woods is a grand passacaglia.

II. L'AME EN PEINE

He sat in the garden,
The soul in pain.
Always to be a poem,
The soul in pain.

Monsieur François
Couperin and Master
Rabelais sat with him,
The soul in pain.

Perhaps there was sunlight,
Perhaps there was rain.
I mean: "in the garden,"
The soul in pain.

The soul in pain,
The soul in pain.
Always to be a poem,
The soul in pain.

III. L'ARLEQUINE

In medias res, when the gods are drunk
And the heroes weep grave, melodious tears,
My classical Harlequin absconds from the study
Of the laws of the Medes and Persians.

Away from the pedants he dwells in the sea,
The Nightingale cries: thalassa.
Opsis and Melos, the Nightingale cries,
The Nightingale cries: thalassa.

IV. LE ROSSIGNOL EN AMOUR

I sat upon the crimson shore
And sang a bitter threnody
About the Nightingale in love
Who packed his bags and put to sea.

About the Nightingale in love
Who fled the forest's verdant shade,
Because the lady in his song
Was no more than the song he made.

Because the lady in his song
Was neither of the east nor west,
The leaves and flowers had become
The forest of his loneliness.

The leaves and flowers have become
A bitter forest unto me,
Wherefore I, like the Nightingale,
Have packed my bags and put to sea.

LAURA

Apple blossoms
and in the evening,
the evening;
a pressed flower
and a locket of hair.

A swallow that sings
for a scarecrow now,
from a bridge of swords
and a cage of air.

A king that was
and a king that shall be;
a photograph
of a photograph
and a locket of hair.

THE YOUNG VIRGINS DANCING ON THE GREEN

The young virgins, dancing on the green
        to the lydian measures
        that Plato has proscribed—
You cannot always be
A young virgin, dancing on the green.

        To the dolorous rhythm?
The rose house, gone mad with roses
Leaping over trellises,
        mad with nostalgia—
You cannot always be
A young virgin, dancing on the green.

To be riven, to be gathered
Into the distance of the poem,
Under the mountain, the rain on our heads.
Of Autumn, of the morte saison
When I said unto you these words:
You cannot always be
A young virgin, dancing on the green.

SIRVENTES: CONTRA INFANTES

Of the cruelty of children,
children are cruel.
The wanton boys
have torn the fly's wing.
The salamanders
mangled
in the rain.

Of works and days
and the blood squeezed from roses,
swaying
in this tradition
(haec traditio)
over the river
and into the trees.

Of sorrow and
heartache, wouldn't you know?
The ghost in the machine
and the princess of the provinces
boarding the ship
that the song has made.

Of sorrow and heartache,
wouldn't you know.
And of the hollow horns,
the vagrant shells
that have laid aside
forgotten vanities.

THE DAYS BECAME THE NIGHTS

The days became the nights
And the nights became a dream

Until a petal fell
And floated in the stream

Above the tattered flesh
The restless moon goes by

Because the soul has wings
It shall not cease to fly

THE HORSEMEN

The moon casts their shadows on the sand
as the waves roll in against the shore;
and what they are is what they think they are,
for what they think they are shall be the same:
a knight with a lance at his side
and a monk in a cowl,
whose horses make steadily their way
down to their pilgrimage in the sea.

And as the two men speak their shadows speak,
for what the horsemen say shall be the same,
as the moon casts their shadows on the sand
and the waves roll in against the shore:
but the shadows of the shadows shall be lost—
they are lost in the midst of the sea.

to Eugene Winchester

THE FISHERMAN AND HIS SOUL

after Oscar Wilde

The river rose, and the Sphinx lay still,
And the swallows flew out among the pyramids.
That he crawls in the morning,
walks upright at noon,
That he sleeps the great sleep in the evening.

And he lived in the Palace of Sans Souçi,
and if pleasure be happiness
under the aegis of the gods,
And that is if pleasure be happiness.
But there's one thing more marvellous still,
And that is the great suffering of the world.

For what men call the shadow of the body
is not the shadow of the body,
but the body of the soul.
And he stood on the shore, and he cut away his shadow,
And the soul went weeping over the marshes.

And what men call the mirrors of wisdom
are not the mirrors of wisdom,
but the mirrors of opinion.
This only is the mirror of wisdom,
For it reflects all things
Save him alone who looks inside it.

And I have hidden this mirror in a cave,
And is there anything better than wisdom?
     Pleasure is better,
     said the young fisherman,
And he stood on the shore, and he dove into the sea,
And the soul went weeping over the marshes.

The river rose, and the Sphinx lay still,
And the swallows flew out among the pyramids.
     That he crawls in the morning,
     walks upright at noon,
That he sleeps the great sleep in the evening.

AB LA DOLCHOR

As the Cypress leans over the Weeping Willow,
Not once thinking of laughter or grief,
Of rain or of the dream of rain,
The Forest of Strangers returning to sleep;
So I lay among women by olive groves;
The moon cast their shadows on the sand
As the waves rolled in against the shore;
Ab la dolchor, and in the sweetness of the new time.

As the Hart thirsts after the Fountains of Water,
Not once thinking of body or mind,
Of pain or of the dream of pain,
The shaft of the Huntsman being lodged in his side;
So my heart thirsted after Thee, O Lord;
Calm was the day, and through the trembling air
The wind in the willows was sweet with Thy word;
Ab la dolchor, and in the sweetness of the new time.

As the Nightingale sings to the Forest of Strangers,
Not once thinking of pity or fear,
Of fame or of the dream of fame,
The sonnet traversing the tides of the years;
So I sang from a chamber of the Solitary Tower:
The exploits of heroes were sung in provençal,
The Redcrosse knight, who was he? George;
Ab la dolchor, and in the sweetness of the new time.

As the Phoenix goes forth as a song from the pyre,
Not once thinking of darkness or light,
Of shame or of the dream of shame,
The prayers of the body consumed in the night;
So my songs went forth after Thee, O Lord;
The moon pulled my shadow into the world,
As the word was made flesh, so the flesh was made word;
Ab la dolchor, and in the sweetness of the new time.

THE BOOK OF SIR TRISTRAM

Of Tristram's long deceased woes

                     the Golden Age
                     is always of the past

The leaves to gold, the moss to red

                     dust on the verdant floor

And how that a life was but a flower

                     the blue tower
                     arose from the sea

Of Tristram's long deceased woes

A WORDSWORTHIAN DREAM IN BLANK VERSE

I was in Rome, and yet it was not Rome:
No yellow Tiber but a turquoise sea
Beneath me flowed, from where I stood upon
The promontory of one of those famed hills,
The seven hills of Rome. I was in Rome.
It was the hour at which the light, grown dim,
Eviscerates the gloom with purple bands
In memory of the sun, which heretofore
Had shone that day in Rome. It was the hour
At which the moon might rise upon the sea,
Startling its ripples with a silver hue
Of highlights flashing, in a moment gone.
And so it was at that same hour in Rome.
There was a fountain, marble in its base,
Whose cold metallic density was framed,
As if suspended in the humid air,
Against the blackened hills, the purpled sky.
Though jets of water rose up from its source,
And rose and fell and rose and fell again,
They seemed to make the stillness yet more still.
I was alone, yet I was not alone;
For standing high above that turquoise sea,
Beside the fountain and beneath the sky,
I seemed to see myself from far away
Climbing the hills of Rome. I was alone,
And yet towards myself I seemed to climb.

It was I, and yet it was not I
Who seemed to hold a book in front of me,
Upon whose spine, emblazoned all in gold,
Was written, *The Mysterious Barricades.*
Whose pages, like the sea, were colored blue;
Whose ink was black and purpled like the sky;
And like the fountain, marble in its base,
Whose words seemed white that rose and fell again,
And rose and fell as if they were my own,
Though none that I had ever read before.
It was I, and yet it was not I.
It seemed to be an ancient tale of Rome.

   I was in Rome, and yet it was not Rome:
No yellow Tiber but a turquoise sea
Beneath me flowed, from where I stood upon
The promontory of one of those famed hills,
The seven hills of Rome.

GRAMMATICAL VERSES

THE DOLOROUS WOOD

Distinguo.
I distinguish between the two cases:
The bird of the forest and the bird of the poem.
The Nightingale flies in the poem,
The Dolorous Wood,
Not Mother Nature's forest,
Hovering th'ambiguous foliage.

Nor does he fly as a symbol,
Perched on a Golden Bough,
As metaphor or allegory
Or as messenger between the realms.
There are no messengers between the realms,
And I distinguish between the two cities:
The Nightingale flies in the poem,
For the song that he sings is himself.

And when the Phoenix is burnt on the pyre,
Does he rise as a myth among men?
And are there any reasons?
The circles converge
Not on the singer but the song.
The ashes are lost in the wind,
And the song goes forth from the flame,
And there are no reasons.

And therefore, distinguo.
I distinguish between the two grammars:
The sphere of the singer and the sphere of the song.
The Phoenix goes forth from the pyre
As a song in the midst of the world,
And he fashions these verses out of nothing
In order that you might remember

to Northrop Frye

XERXES

The king and the rose,
                    the young king
                                    and the rose,
would kneel him down
                    before a rose,
                                Ombra mai fu:
and that was Xerxes the tenor
                    in Handel's Largo—

not as at Salamis,
                    nor yet as in the alphabet-book:

X is for Xerxes,
                    the mad king—
                                    which you play upon the piano —
the whole world
                    within the skein of a progression,

a history of sadness
                    in the thread of a common memory—

I, who have always
                    been a shadow.
                                Ombra mai fu:
and that politics be music,
                    as the Poet King has written,

that the circles converge
                    not on the battle
                                    but the dance

which is Xerxes—
        the measure of our lives

strung between the poles
        of a double symmetry—

in and out of existence
        or passing through a mirror,

I, who have always been
        Xerxes,
        the poem and the man—
I, who have always
        been a shadow.
        Ombra mai fu:
and that this be the history
        which is graven on our lives,

the beauty and the madness
        and the seven ambiguities:

you send for the oracle
        but the ships come back empty—

they descend into history
        from whence you arose—

and you do not go
        forth
        across the Hellespont,

you remain as a metaphor,
                      a twittering shade

strung between the poem
               and the world--
                         Xerxes, Xerxes,
you are mostly unknown
               and accustomed to sorrow--

and that this be the history
               which is graven on our lives.

The king and the rose,
             the young king
                    and the rose,
would kneel him down
             before a rose,
                  Ombra mai fu:
let the circles converge
             upon the poem
                  till at last you return,
and let this be your history,
             your paradise
                  terrestre,
here and in Persia
          your land of heart's desire.

JESUS OF NAZARETH, THE KING OF THE JEWS

I am not the poem, but was sent to bear
        witness of the poem
that shineth in darkness, and the darkness
        comprehendeth it not—
I have written what I have written.

Nor am I the poet, which is only the
        metaphor of the poem,
the demiurge of darkness, who cometh between
        the poem and the man—
I have written what I have written.

I made a title, and put it on the poem,
        and the writing was
JESUS OF NAZARETH, THE KING OF THE JEWS—
I have written what I have written.

This was not the poem, and yet it
        became the poem,
the one who suffered, the one who was there—
I have written what I have written.

to William Bronk

THE LIVES OF THE POETS

Dying his life, living his death,
Chatterton starved that Rowley might breathe.
The lives of the poets are my life—
I am the lives of the poets.

Homer was blind. The rosy-fingered Dawn,
Who rises in the east from Tithon's throne
Spreading her beams upon the wine-dark Sea,
Was but an epithet to hold his memory.
And what was Troy? Homer invented Troy.
Troy was a name, a landscape in the mind
Of someone we call Homer, who was blind.

The lives of the poets are my life—
I am the lives of the poets.

Dante, who lived in Hell, conceived of bliss
Through Beatrice—but who was Beatrice?
She was a little girl, a Florentine
Whom he had met when she was eight or nine.
The Earl of Surrey calls her Geraldine,
Tracing her lineage from the Tuscan line
Of Petrarch's Laura—Laura, for the air
Which, being anguished, echoed his despair.

The lives of the poets are my life—
I am the lives of the poets.

Shakespeare (as in the well known parable
By Señor Borges) was invisible.
At Stratford-on-Avon he built himself a house,
And there he lived and died—anonymous.
He was not Hamlet, nor was meant to be
The heroic figure of a tragedy
Whose life becomes the symbol for an age—
Because he disappeared into his page.

The lives of the poets are my life—
I am the lives of the poets.

Shelley was drowned. The night before he died,
He wrote these words: "Then what is life? I cried."
The triumph of life is the lofty pride
Of a luminous angel—wings against the void.
For Shelley and Shakespeare and Chatterton,
And Homer and Dante—all are forms of one
Spiritual life unfolding in time,
Whose essence is light, whose motion is in rhyme.

The lives of the poets are my life—
I am the lives of the poets.

ADAM AND EVE

Because it is perfect, it encompasses us. Then why
do we think always of what lies beyond its boundaries?
And having become conscious that what they evoke
is ourselves, we begin to yearn for something
which is only a dim intuition: its location
unknown to us—far beyond the reaches of experience.

Far beyond the reaches of experience, we imagine
ourselves there, having invented the power to imagine.
And with no other images, how should we imagine ourselves
but as we are? We think of ourselves as being
there, and it is perfect because it encompasses us.

The World was all before them, where to choose
Thir place of rest, and Providence thir guide

Because it no longer encompasses us, we think
back upon that time—when we were there.
And having become conscious that what we have lost
is ourselves, we begin to grieve for something
which is always behind us, and as we go forward
to where we are not—far beyond the reaches of experience.

Far beyond the reaches of experience, we remember
ourselves there, having invented the power to remember.
And with no other memories, how should we remember ourselves
but as we are? We think of ourselves as being
there, and it is perfect because it encompasses us.

They looking back, all th'Eastern side beheld
Of Paradise, so late thir happy seat

Because it can never encompass us, we are always
alone, we inhabit the spaces before us.
And having become conscious that all that there is
is ourselves, we begin to think of the world
as the meditation for desires that give birth to themselves,
unfolding—far beyond the reaches of experience.

Far beyond the reaches of experience, we are conscious
of ourselves as the boundaries of our own self-consciousness.
And with no other boundaries, how should we be conscious of ourselves
but as we change? We think of ourselves as becoming
ourselves, and as encompassing what lies beyond us.

They hand in hand with wand'ring steps and slow,
Through Eden took thir solitary way.

THE UNICORN TAPESTRIES

I

Bereft of nature, consciousness must weave
A tapestry of loss through which to grieve;
Through loss to find itself, through death to live.

For consciousness, arising from the womb
Of nature, natureless, is its own tomb:
Unless the skein be woven on the loom,

It is a ghost that does but weave the wind.
And history, which is the struggle of the mind
To realize itself, can only find
Itself through nature, which as such is blind

Until, renatured in antithesis
And conscious of itself as consciousness,
It sees itself in what is imageless.

II

Seeking itself, through its activity
To subsume nature into subjectivity,
Freedom must itself endure captivity

And dissolution through its sufferings.
It must be torn asunder by the slings
And arrows of outrageous priests and kings,
Whose creed is, 'No ideas but in things',

Because its truth is antithetical
To nature. It must be deemed heretical
And crowned with thorns, enclosed behind a wall

Of terror, falsehood and perversity.
All this must freedom of necessity
Endure, for thus it comes itself to be.

III

To be is but the form of to desire,
And spirit, though its breath the flames inspire,
Wherewith it is consumed on its own pyre,
Shall not forbear to fulminate the fire

Because it lights the passage to its womb.
To be is but the form of to become,
And spirit, though it come upon the tomb

Of all it was and all it once enjoyed,
Shall not forbear to be itself destroyed
Because it is upborne against the void.

To be is but the form of to be free,
And spirit, though its wings loose entropy
Upon itself, shall not forbear to fly.

IV

Because its flight is fate, because its fate
Unfolds through what it labors to create,
Time forms the state, and yet it flies the state

Of things as they are. For how should time attain
Unto itself, if things as they are remain?
It would be turned into a beast again,

And as a beast to nothingness descend.
Because it seeks itself to comprehend,
Therefore must time the things of time transcend

Until such time as time shall cease to be--
When having passed into eternity,
It recapitulates its destiny;
For then the state shall wither, and so die.

ENVOI

TO CHRISTINE

Go, Song, and sing to Music, for she weeps
At your departure, she is filled with pain;
She that has borne you sleeps alone again,
Her dreams unknown—then go to where she sleeps
That, singing, you may enter in her soul;
Return to her a lover, cast your seed
In that sweet garden where you first were bred,
And where, conjoined, you both again are whole.
The generations struggle to be born!
They all cry out to Music from the womb,
That she convey them to the destined home
Where they shall come to Music in their turn.
Then go, Song, sing to Music, for she longs
For you to come and water her with songs.

Henry Weinfield was born in Montreal, Canada in 1949. He holds degrees from the City College of New York, where he was an editor of *Promethean Magazine*, and the State University of New York at Binghamton. *The Carnival Cantata*, his first collection of poems, was published by Unicorn Press in 1971. Between 1972 and 1976, he edited *The Mysterious Barricades*, a journal of the arts. Henry Weinfield lives in New York City.

Henry Weinfield